C000137262

Hat

Bl

B L O O M S B U R Y
LONDON • NEW DELHI • NEW YORK • SYDNEY

Bloomsbury Methuen Drama
An imprint of Bloomsbury Publishing Plc

50 Bedford Square	1385 Broadway
London	New York
WC1B 3DP	NY 10018
UK	USA

www.bloomsbury.com

Bloomsbury is a registered trade mark of Bloomsbury Publishing Plc

First published 2014

British Library Cataloguing-in-Publication Data
A catalogue record for this book is available from the British Library.

ISBN: PB: 978-1-4725-6879-3
ePub: 978-1-4725-6878-6
ePDF: 978-1-4725-6877-9

Library of Congress Cataloging-in-Publication Data
A catalog record for this book is available from the Library of Congress.

Typeset by Mark Heslington Ltd, Scarborough, North Yorkshire
Printed and bound in Great Britain

Bluebeard

by Hattie Naylor

GALLIVANT...

Joint Artistic Directors Hattie Naylor and Lee Lyford make theatre collaboratively, alongside Creative Associates Paul Dodgson and Hayley Grindle. *Bluebeard* launches their company *Gallivant*.

Gallivant combine text, design, sound, and physicality into one seamless whole and create theatre that is fabulist in tradition, where comedy and darkness entertain with equal depth and seduction.

Bluebeard was first performed June 2013 at Bristol Old Vic Studio, enabled by Bristol Old Vic Ferment.

Original Production

Bluebeard	**Paul Mundell**
Writer	**Hattie Naylor**
Director	**Lee Lyford**
Composer and Sound Designer	**Paul Dodgson**
Set and Costume Designer	**Hayley Grindle**
Producer	**Katherine Lazare**
Producer	**Kerrie Avery**
Lighting Designer	**Ben Dodds**
Stage Manager	**Alicia White**
Director of Possibility (Trailer & Website Design)	**Tom Brereton Downs**
Graphic Design	**www.whitespace-brand.co.uk**
Logo Design	**Michael Cranston**

Note from **Gallivant**

There has been a consistent disregard for feminist values for some time, epitomised in the recent argument with Facebook regarding female imagery, the proliferation of violent pornography, and even in so called 'mommy porn' like *Fifty Shades of Grey*. We wanted to make a piece that questions us, the audience, and our complicity in the acts that Bluebeard commits. Why are we titillated by this? And is this OK? It is not so much an attack on violence in entertainment or pornography as such but a provocation that questions our complicity with it. We have allowed this material to slip under our radar unchallenged and despite women being more equal on a surface level, subtly we find women are in a considerably worse position than they were 20 years ago, and they have possibly been complicit in letting it happen.

Gallivant would like to thank:

George Lasha, Tom Morris, Sharon Clark, Lina B Frank and Emma Bettridge and all at Bristol Old Vic, for supporting, developing and enabling the realisation of this production. Simon Day and Theatre Bristol. Phil Hindson, Tom Downs, Sarah-Jayne White, Jordan Whyte, Bethany Hocken, Jessica MacDonald, Gemma Brooks and Chris Samuels. Kate Cross and her team at the egg. Giles Smart and Nicki Stoddart at United Agents. Nina Steiger, Steve Marmion, Joe Murphy, and all at the Soho Theatre. Dan, Richard, Sharon and the rest of the team at Mobius Industries.

Hattie would like to thank Tim Crouch for the inspirational *The Author*.

www.gallivant.org.uk

Kerrie Avery (Producer)

Kerrie Avery is an Associate Producer at Theatre Bristol and has developed her freelance practice through collaboration with Gallivant (*Bluebeard*); MAYK and Mayfest Bristol (2011 ongoing); Dreadnought South West (*Oxygen*); Jen Bell (*Temple Songs* and *In a Town*) and Kaleider (*Invisible Flock, Bring the Happy*). Working for Mayfest she has worked alongside various national and international artists and companies including Kate Tempest and Battersea Arts Centre (*Brand New Ancients*); Andy Field (*Motor Vehicle Sundown*); Banana Bag & Bodice (*Beowulf*); Clod Ensemble (*Zero*); John Moran (*Goodbye Thailand*); National Theatre of Wales and Neon Neon (*Praxis Makes Perfect*); SKaGen (*Bigmouth*); Ontroerend Goed (*All That Is Wrong*); Little Bulb Theatre (*Operation Greenfield* and *Goose Party*); Darren Johnston (*Ousia*); Search Party (*Save Me*) and Bryony Kimmings (*Sex Idiot*).

Having a wide range of experience in producing and project management in theatre, live music, touring, site-specific productions, public space works, television and live events, Kerrie has developed a considered and knowledgeable practice for producing creatively admired projects both in the UK and Internationally. She has considerable financial management, public consultation and reporting experience across a broad range of arts practices.

Tom Brereton Downs – Director of Possibility (Trailer & Website Design)

Tom loves to help creative people and organisations feel great, look great and do great things. He thinks realism is overrated and optimism underrated. His 'how can we' approach has seen him help launch a music college in Berlin, open a chain of ten shops for a British artist and recruit Richard E. Grant, Rebecca Hall and Penelope Keith for his promotional film about a regional theatre. He is currently on a mission to build the Facebook of art.

Ben Dodds (Lighting Designer)

Ben is a freelance Lighting Designer and Production Electrician, having recently left the National Theatre where he was a Senior Lighting Technician. At the National, he has assisted the lighting designer on productions of *Every Good Boy Deserves Favour*, *De Profundis*, *England People Very Nice* and *War Horse* among many others. He has also done re-lights for the NT: *One Man, Two Guvnors* UK and international tour, as well as for DV8 Physical Theatre on *Can We Talk About This*. Other touring roles include production electrician on the NT tour of *Hamlet*. Professional lighting design credits include *These Things Happen* at the Courtyard Theatre, *The Revolution Will Be Sexual* at the Arcola, Watch This Space festival at the NT and Future Cinema's production of *Grease*, as well as numerous event and festival designs.

Paul Dodgson (Music/Composer)

Paul is a writer, composer/sound designer, radio producer and teacher. Theatre work includes music/lyrics/sound design for productions of *Heidi – A Goat's Tale*, *The French Detective and the Blue Dog* and *The Nutcracker* (Theatre Royal Bath); *Alice Through the Looking Glass* (Tobacco Factory Bristol); *The Kingdom* (Soho Theatre); *Joking Apart* (Nottingham Playhouse) and *The Importance of Being Earnest* and *Way Upstream* (Salisbury Playhouse). He has written and produced twelve plays for BBC Radio 4 including *You Drive Me Crazy*, *Binge Drunk Britain – The Musical* and *Windscale*. Screenwriting credits include eighteen months as part of the *EastEnders* writing team and the drama/documentary series *Monsters We Met* for BBC 2. Paul has recently taught creative writing at Exeter University where he previously held a two-year post as Writer-in-Residence specialising in life-writing, a genre he now teaches internationally.

Hayley Grindle (Set and Costume Design)

Hayley Grindle is a London based Theatre Designer who graduated from the Royal Welsh College of Music and Drama in 2002.

Since then Hayley has continued to design productions across the UK, and extensively at the Theatre Royal Bath.

Theatre includes *Cooking With Elvis* (Derby Theatre); *Arabian Nights*, *Bluebeard* (Gallivant); *All The Way Home* (Manchester Library Theatre); *Mongrel Island*, *The Boy Who Fell Into A Book* (Soho Theatre); *Animal Farm* (The Peter Hall Company); *Heidi, The Nutcracker*, *Around the World in Eighty Days*, *Ben Hur*, *His Dark Materials*, *Blue Room*, *A Midsummer Night's Dream* (all Theatre Royal Bath); *God in Ruins* (RSC); *Little Voice*, *My Mother Said I Never Should*, *Peter Pan* (The Dukes, Lancaster); *Invisible* and *As You Like It* (Transport Theatre); *Travels With My Aunt* (New Wolsey, Ipswich); *The Gentlemen's Tea Drinking Society* (Ransom Productions, Belfast); *Muscle* (Bristol Old Vic/Hull Truck); *Two Shakespearean Actors*, *A Midsummer Night's Dream* (Guildhall Drama School); *The Mikado* (Welsh National Youth Opera); *Bob, the Man on the Moon* (Travelling Light); *Treasure Island* (Watermill Theatre, Newbury); *Invisible* (a co-production between Transport and the New Wolsey Ipswich); *Of Mice and Men*, *The Strange Case of Dr Jekyll and Mr Hyde* (The Watermill); *Ball Room of Joys and Sorrows* (Kate Flatt and Watford Palace Theatre); *The Private Ear and The Public Eye* (Original Theatre); *Fantastic Mr Fox* (Singapore Repertory Theatre).

Recipient of the Paul Kimpton Prize for Innovation (RWCMD).

Recently nominated by Manchester Theatre Awards for best design for *Arabian Nights*.

Forthcoming productions include *Robin Hood* (Manchester Library Theatre); *All My Sons* (The Watermill), *A Taste of Honey* (Hull Truck).

Since then Hayley has continued to design productions across the UK, and extensively at The Theatre Royal Bath.

Katherine Lazare (Producer)

Katherine works at Theatre Royal Bath as part of the producing team for the egg. This is where she has collaborated with Lee, Hattie, Hayley and Paul on many productions.

Katherine has produced over forty productions with the Theatre Royal Bath's Young People's Theatre (YPT). The YPT were a partner for the National Theatre's Connections programme in 2004 and 2006. From 2003 to 2009 Katherine produced a co-commissioning programme with the American Conservatory Theater, San Francisco, working with writers including Sharman MacDonald, Sarah Daniels and Ursula Rani Sarma. She produces Theatre Royal Bath's annual summer production *Storm on the Lawn*, and is part of the team developing theatre for young audiences under the egg's Leverhulme and Esmee Fairbairn Incubator programme.

Katherine has also worked as a Director, Workshop Leader, and Stage Manager.

Lee Lyford (Director/Joint Artistic Director)

Plays directed at the Theatre Royal Bath and the egg include *Heidi – A Goat's Tale* (ad. Andrew Pollard); *The Judgement of Macbeth* (Hattie Naylor); *The French Detective and the Blue Dog* (Hattie Naylor); *Alice Through the Looking Glass* (ad. Hattie Naylor); *Ben Hur* (ad. Hattie Naylor); *His Dark Materials* (ad. Nicholas Wright); *Peter Pan*, *Around the World in Eighty Days* (ad.Toby Hulse); *Guys And Dolls*, *A Midsummer Night's Dream*, *My Life As A Fairytale* (Hattie Naylor); *Broken Hallelujah* (Sharman Macdonald); *Broken Wings* (Sarah Daniels); *War Daddy* (Jim Grimsley); *The Nutcracker* (ad. Hattie Naylor); *My Life In The Silents* (Timothy Mason); *The Odyssey* (ad. Hattie Naylor); *Animal Farm* (ad. Peter Hall)

Plays directed for other organisations include *Muscle* (Tom Wainwright) for Bristol Old Vic and Hull Truck

Movement Direction includes *The Witch Of Edmonton* (Southwark Playhouse); *Fen/Far Away* (Sheffield Crucible); *When Harry Met Sally* (national tour); *Mother Savage* (Travelling Light). Choreography includes *We're Going On A Bear Hunt* (Bristol Old Vic); *The Ugly Duckling* (Tobacco Factory and Travelling Light).

Lee is the egg Associate Director.

Paul Mundell (Bluebeard)

Paul trained at Bristol Old Vic Theatre School.

Theatre credits include *The French Detective and the Blue Dog* (Theatre Royal Bath, the egg); *Flies* (Pins and Needles and Tobacco Factory Bristol); *Muscle* (Hull Truck and Bristol Old Vic); *Alice Through the Looking Glass* (Theatre Royal Bath, the egg); *Spyski* (Peepolykus/Lyric Hammersmith); *A Christmas Carol* and *Alice Through the Looking Glass* (Tobacco Factory, Bristol); *Beauty and The Beast* (Creation Theatre Company); *Kindertransport* (Aberystwyth Arts Centre); *Can of Worms* (Strange Bedfellows/BAC); *Fallen Angels* (Big State Theatre); *The Chronicles of Hoggett & Webb* (Innerroom Theatre Company); *Eggshell Blues* (Theatre West); *Twelfth Night* and *Hamlet* (Cambridge Shakespeare Festival) and *The Picture of Dorian Gray* (Big Telly Theatre Company) and *Come Rain, Come Shine* (The Shakespeare Revue Company).

Film credits include *Small Talk*, *The Sad Case*, *The Call*, and *Hammered*.

Television credits include *Inside the Titanic* (Dangerous Films Ltd/ Discovery/Channel 5).

Radio includes *The Martin Beck Killings*, *The Quest*, *Anaesthesia*, *Faust*, *On The Field*, *Cavity*, *Perfect Day*, *J'Accuse* and *Poetry Please* (all BBC Radio 4).

Hattie Naylor (Writer/Joint Artistic Director)

Hattie is an award winning writer and co-founder of the company Gallivant. She was studying painting at the Slade School of Art when her first play was accepted in the BBC Radio Young Playwrights Festival. She has won several national and international awards for her plays and has had over 40 plays, three short stories, and an opera broadcast on BBC Radio 4 and/or 3.

Ivan and the Dogs for Soho Theatre with ATC was nominated in the 2010 Olivier Awards for Outstanding Achievement, the radio version of *Ivan and the Dogs*, directed and edited by Paul Dodgson, won the Tinniswood Award for Best Original Radio Drama in 2009. The play is about to go on the syllabus and has been translated into seven languages with new productions in New York, Tbilisi, Athens, Barcelona, Rotterdam, Sao Paulo, Rio de Janeiro, and Buenos Aires.

Other productions include the opera *Piccard in Space* composer Will Gregory (Goldfrapp) for the Southbank and Radio 3, conducted by Charles Hazlewood and directed by Jude Kelly, QEH April 2010, *Mother Savage* directed by Craig Edwards, and *The Nutcracker* co-written with Paul Dodgson, and directed by Lee Lyford for Theatre Royal Bath. Recent work include *The French Detective and the Blue Dog* with Paul Dodgson, directed by Lee Lyford for the egg, the current serialisation of *The Diaries of Samuel Pepys,* and *The Aeneid* both for BBC Radio 4 directed by Kate McAll, and *Going Dark* with Sound&Fury, directed by Dan Jones and Mark and Tom Espiner, Critics Choice in both the Guardian and Time Out, London, Young Vic, 2012 and touring next year.

This Christmas (2013) *Moominland Midwinter* will be at the egg Theatre Royal Bath directed by Lee Lyford and Alison Duddle for Horse and Bamboo, and *The Nutcracker* will be at the Nuffield Theatre directed by Blanche McIntyre.

Alicia White (Stage Manager)
Alicia trained at the Royal Welsh College of Music and Drama and is now working as a Freelance Stage Manager. Previous credits include DSM, *Jumpers for Goalposts* by Tom Wells (Paines Plough and Hull Truck); DSM, *Out Of Their Minds* (the egg, Theatre Royal Bath); SM, *Cwtch Cabaret* (Citrus Arts); ASM, *Prometheus* (Secret Cinema). Whilst predominantly working in theatre, Alicia also has experience of events. She has recently worked as Artist Liaison/Stage Manager on the Big Splash Festival: a circus, cabaret and street theatre festival in Newport, Wales. Alicia collaborated with Lee Lyford on the egg's production of The Queen's Knickers at the Southbank Centre in 2013. Alicia is CSM on book for Tom Well's *Jumpers for Goalposts* national UK tour and Bush Theatre 2013.

www.gallivant.org.uk

© Paul Blakemore

© Paul Blakemore

Paul Mundell in *Bluebeard* at Bristol Old Vic Studio, June 2013 © Paul Blakemore

Bluebeard

Bluebeard   I won't call it cunt, or pussy, or twat,
I'll call it red.

Her red.

I won't call it cock, or dick, or nob,

I'll call it granite, my granite.

I won't call them breasts, or tits, or baps.

I'll call them her selves – her little selves –
heaving up and down
beneath: a blouse, a shirt, a thin cotton dress
with tiny pearl buttons down the front
of
it. (*Refers to her.*)

* * *

Susan was from Burnley.
Thin, white, gentle, dull. Twenty-two, twenty-
four, maybe younger,
nineteen. Perhaps. I can't really remember.

She knew.

There at the bottom of her, of her thin white,
gentle, dull, green eyed self, was it,
this . . .
like a small flame.

Not so dull close up – was Susan.

Who had a Mum, a Dad and a brother – friends,
was
liked.

I was walking. Out and about.
I spotted, watched, followed then fell over,
near her. My knee cut.
She helps. Produces a plaster from her bag.

The gentle cannot resist giving help to the
hurt.

I say 'I'm lost'.
She says 'Where d'you want to get to?'
I smile. She blinks.
I say 'I was walking on the moors. Now I am
terribly lost. But you must let me thank you for
helping me.'

And in the blinking, immediate, total desire of
her initially dull self she says
'Well, alright.'
And I guide her to a café and then a bar.

She is snow white, a beauty.

There's a date.
At the cinema.

I place my arm around the back of her seat.
It's a horror film.
When she's afraid she curls into me
and I laugh, quietly, gently –
and stroke her hair.
She does this again and again –
curling up in horror, holding onto me –
as she gasps – giggling after the 'fright of it'.
Yet she chose the film.

Any woman that has had sex with more than
one man in the film dies horribly – is broken
and mutilated.
And the audience groans and giggles in fear
and titillation, as body meets chainsaw

and fake blood pours from severed limbs.
Afterwards I take her to a restaurant and
we laugh at the decapitated, and imaginative
deaths.

And I kiss her.

I bring gifts, always bring gifts.
Her eyes widen. None of the very few others –
maybe there has only been one, maybe two, no
one brought gifts. Something carefully chosen
– encircled with the promise of love.

I bring a bell from Tibet.
I cup it in my hand.
I run its stick round the side
gently but firmly, never losing contact.
The bell begins to sound.
The harmonics form a long transcendent note,
it is transfixing, unbelievably beautiful – and
penetrates everything, everything
reverberates.
It's from an ancient valley, thick with green
undergrowth, half in mist, so very cold in the
morning, the white tops of the mountains just
in view.

The sound carries this world,

this ancient paradise.

Susan has never been given anything as

wondrous.

It's a winner.

And I kiss her hard, differently now from

before – I hold the back of her neck, I lace my

fingers around her hair, I pull – slightly, so her

head is back, I am upon her with my tongue

curled in her mouth. I let go.

We drive out to look at the moors.

The rain and mist is thick.

She is cold.

We sit inside the car.

The wind rocks us slightly.

Howls about us.

We are a tiny, tiny thing surrounded by violent

nature.

And there I stroke the line of her, I guide my

hand down her neck, down the centre of her,

then across her little selves, with the backs of

my fingers, and then down to her waist, and

down again, down her back to her legs and
then thighs, tracing my fingers across them
and then up to the very edge of her.
And I leave it there.
Pull away.
I watch desire smelt her – fold her into a
different shape. She is melting inside.

She smells of love. She is dreamy with it. She
shines from head to toe.
She gleams. And her little selves heave and
sigh inside her tiny tight top, and she blinks
half innocent, half not, with an eye on the dark
corner of the room.
The faint trace of abuse already marked across
her skin.
She'll want to go back there. I am certain of it.
She'll want to attempt to understand it,
however slight that terrible wrong was.

And we meet again and this time she wears a
top with small pearl buttons down the front
and a short cotton skirt. And I kiss her, stroke
her, pet her, and then take my hand across her

selves and one by one undo the buttons with
my fingers, I lay my hands across her, hold her
little selves in my hands, suck and squeeze and
kiss, then bite. Holding her selves between my
teeth. She sighs.

And then my hand moves down to her legs,
pushing her thighs apart.

And my fingers find her red – and push gently
at the very beginning of her and then harder
and harder – inside – furious for her. She likes
the fury. And she sighs and longs for it and
loves.

Then again – I stop – I make her wait.

And we meet again.

I make her strip – each piece removed without
my touching – just a command, a simple order.

He visualises her gradually undressing.

Top,
now skirt,
underwear
no.
Top again. Yes that now. Let me see them.

No, slowly, slowly.

Now below.

Slowly. Susan, look at me.

Look at me.

Take it off so it edges across your skin.

So I can see all of you gradually – bit by bit.

Reveal your nakedness to me slowly.

There.

There now.

That's perfect.

And she is standing in front of.

Her white form is naked. All of her.

Then I put her on the bed and lay my fingers across her.

Wooing her body still – gentle for one more moment.

I tie her down. And wait. I tease her body. I torment her.

Till the longing is an all consuming ache.

Till every part of her begs for me.

Only then I take her –

a rock against her – like stone against her –

cold and ferocious – raging in and out of her.

Again and again. Deep inside.

And she acquiesces to every moment. Her ties

hurt her, my fury hurts her, my positioning

hurts her, the foulness of all that I do – the

degradation – every hole, every pain, all the

imaginably re-lived horrors

in lines of hurt across the skin. But she excels

in this – she loves all this – Susan from Burnley

is ecstatic – in bliss.

There is nothing, you understand like pain,

like hurt,

nothing like that.

Nothing compares. Ask anyone.

But it goes on.

We are an item now.

Susan and I.

And steadily and certainly it escalates.

The ferocity with which she extracts violent

desire and her need for pain, is endless –

inflicted upon her tiny white self as endless as

my desire to wreck her.

The more I claim my freedom the more she
becomes un-free.
I want to destroy everything.

I tie her up again and repeatedly beat her, she
sighs, naked and bruised, she delights at my
brutality. I own her and she wants to be owned.
She laughs, the marks, the bruises – the place
of abuse
re-lived – Susan from Burnley is happy.

Silence.

Then she begins to dig.
She wanted to know it all.
Family, friends,
country
food for Christ's sake.

And childhood.

Everything dug and dug.
But I showed her
slowly painfully,
dragged a knife against her naked skin.

Dragged its silver edge down the middle,

between her selves, just touching the flesh –

the cold knife against her. The metal – makes

her shiver.

She giggles like a half child woman.

The granite is hard as rock

but this time – I make her white flesh shudder.

I made her red, redder. And the games reach

their climax – as they always do.

She is naked in the earth.

She is screaming.

* * *

Now let's not pity me.

Let's say I had a happy childhood.

Let's say I had a normal one. Nothing went

wrong.

Let's say this 'innate'.

It came with birth.

It was always there. Let's say it's the way I

always was.

Or we can say this.

If we're saying it can't be innate. Couldn't be.

Let's say that some of us have had cruel and

unspeakable acts committed against us when

young – let's say that of me – for a moment.

But only some then turn out this way.

Why so few?

Which way is easier, for the viewer, listener,

participant?

Nature does not come with moral guidelines,

the weak are crushed by her. Tyranny is nature

– in the bedroom and in all things. Mouth

against cunt, finger in red, her red, red self,

the right of my granite to claim every part,

every hole. The right to my freedom.

Because it was, is, for me innate.

No one showed me what to do.

It came like a dream

Here (*Refers to head.*) of its own volition.

Full of its own pure, uncluttered, nature.

My nature

Is

This.

And women find flesh steeped in the threat of
violence, irresistible. Smelling of it. And even if
you don't ever court *'the Brute'*, on that good
and wise day –
I, speaking for me, have never, ever found it
hard to attract the ladies. They fall
smitten
always and forever. It's easy.

And Susan is now begging. Her beaten white
self, bloody and bruised against the dark earth,
raped and denied all charity. But this is my
favourite thing – to see a woman weep and I
always make women weep. There is nothing
here but annihilation and this moment only.
Where death encases life.

I have restored both Susan and I to the vicious
state of nature.

Susan is still screaming. And I am still thrusting
into her and then my moment of timeless total
annihilation – comes, when her pain is at its
most painful, and time stops for my solitary

footsteps in heaven. I wait, fold myself around
my moment of everything.

There. Just there . . .

I pull out and walk around her, observing her
pain. Watching it. She is dying and now, now,
just now . . .
She is dead.

I clean up and walk away.

We always know the innards of what we court,
fancy, desire –
want to fuck. That's why we find the same
person over and over again.

There's the sad familiar repeating tale of the
girl that finds herself with another brute, then
another, only to find that the last cautiously
chosen lover – dishes a blow so hard one day –
that she's sent hurtling into beyond. Found
weeks later bruised and beaten – senseless,
naked in the earth.

* * *

Then there was Annabel from Hartlepool,
divorced, poised, and agitated. Thirty-nine
and on the cusp.
Uplifting firming creams,
age-defying serums, miracle face packs – lining
her side table – echoing the words 'I'm not
worth it'. Three years on she was still fighting
for an endowment policy and his pension.
Annabel with a sorrow so deep in her soul – so
loud you could hear it, like . . . a distant
solitary bell – 'my life is over, there will be no
grandchildren, no second house on a lonely
moor, no fireside warmth with you, the age of
love is gone, gone, gone'. Annabel was easy.

And experience is a tender and enjoyable thing
to spend time with – with the divorced there is
usually 'no introduction to erotica necessary'.
And like I said, if they like the smell of violence
laced into one's flesh then they'll already have
a knowledge and experience of such.

The seduction needs not to be slow, you
understand,
the initiation into 'the games' does not need to
be so careful.

She was backing out, in her Hyundai Coupe.
She thought it her mistake. Flustered, angry
and sorry. I lit a cigarette and handed it her – I
don't smoke – but always keep a pack for the
panicked. For comfort.

I told her I would make no claim if she gave
me her number.
It made her laugh.
Her wide mouth open, her laser-cleaned teeth,
perfect.
'How much will you charge me if I don't,' – she
asked.
'I don't know' I said – 'maybe a grand – what
with the body work and re-spraying; dusky
cardinal can be a hard red to find.'
She laughs again and gets out her mobile.
'What's yours?' she says. 'I'll ring you now.'

Smiles. Then with real menace.

Easy.

It was Annabel's suggestion I should buy the
club – said with all
my ill-gotten gains – I should invest.
So I did.
Didn't run it – just gave some money – owned
it – I liked the dancing – where you can watch
sex before it happens – made finding them
easier. Much. Northern Soul, fashionable in a
retro kind of way. Lucrative.

Annabel knew, she knew what I was. No
explanation necessary.
The ecstasy of subordination in erotica – was
already well celebrated in Annabel.

I'd guide her to the torture chamber, hand cuff
her, sodomise her, whip her, rape her, leave her
hanging there for hours – howling for more of
me. She loved it.

And for weeks she never asked.
Left me alone.
Never offered her pity.

She was good, for a while.

And then she dug in. Wanted to know it all.
'Yes, yes!' I shouted. 'We were like everybody
else. We drank Cup-a-Soup!'

It's not for you to know about me.

I guide the knife along the surface
against her silk top.
The little selves sighing beneath
my granite hard as rock.
My knife snapping one button off, then
another, cupped and kissed them before I
tipped the cold edge of the knife against her
tiny selves, and down to her thighs and the end
of her.
She thought she could take it.

I made her white flesh shudder.

Silence.

Sometimes I let them live
it depends on the maths –

Whether they will tell.
But most
don't.

Not if they are complicit

and Annabel is,

very complicit.

Even up to the pain she now reels and cries against

she is complicit.

She knows in her heart that 'she asked for it'.

She knows that in the middle of us there is a worthless soul,

a tiny self,

a weak pitying alone self that no one understands, that no one can reach. And alone and misunderstood it craves for its own end. Alone this worthless self craves its end-of-it-all. Why else do we stay with the abuser if only to know again and again – that (*Utterly vulnerable, internal.*) 'I am worthless, I am worthless, I am worthless'.

Smiles.

Plunged in and plundered.

She is on the ground.

Ruined

Desecrated

Too broken to cry out anymore.

And with my 'moment' gone, my skip in
heaven over –

It is not that I have remorse as I look at her
weeping, as I look at her filled.

It is more that I am . . . (*Searching for the right
word.*)

Bored. When there is still so much new
excitement to find.

And she won' t say. Tell.

Because (*Laughing/smiling – of course.*) she is
complicit.

Back to his dark self.

It is certainly time to walk on. To move on to
some other. Yes certainly.

FX MUSIC – The Night by Frankie Valli.

Bluebeard *dances.*

This is all we are. This is all sex is. The
attempted obliteration of the self. That's why
it's so brutal. All there is, is the plane of nature.
It is what was before and will always be, and
our complete annihilation, this leisurely
murdered world, is after all, only what is.

* * *

Back at the club I notice Judy. Watched her on
the floor. Watched her little hips sway back and
forth. Watched her dress cling, her thighs,
waist, her little selves. Watched her dance.

I join her.
Swaying.
We dance together.
I make her laugh.
Ask her out.
She's seen me about.
Noticed me, she says.
It's arranged. She'll come by my flat, she says,
we'll go out from there.

But we don't.
On that first night.
She wears black.
A linen dress.
Striking but
discrete.
Heels,

of course.

Raw silk beneath.

Black, everything black.

Tight about her tiny white form

shaped and cut to fit her every slight curve

holding her tight form in.

I take her coat, edge it across her shoulders,

my fingers brush against her back.

We drink.

Talk.

She tells me she likes lots of different types of

music.

She tells me there is no type of food she

particularly prefers.

I pour more.

She touches my hand, as I pour, nudges

against it.

Then she stands up.

I can see her body twitch slightly beneath her

black attire

so carefully and I suppose obviously chosen.

But still appreciated.

The hours she must have taken deciding,

what I would like

what makes her look so very best

The slight make-up
The grooming
Everything clean.

And here she is,
In my flat.
All silk beneath,
touching her skin,
chiffon against her legs,
up to her pale whiteness.
An unwrapped present.

I put my hand around the back of her neck
and she tilts her head
and we kiss.
Tenderly and sweetly – she unravels.
I push my tongue into her mouth.
I do not wait for Judy.
I cannot resist her.

I unzip her dress, and lift it,
sliding over her thighs, over her hips, and then
held against her,
so she cannot move,
and I slide my hands into

all

that

raw silk and against her red.

I remove layer after layer.

That first night.

The first night we touched.

The first night we fucked.

The first I walked in heaven because of her.

Pause.

And I think of her

often.

She appears in my thoughts

when one is not looking there she is

there is Judy.

Her hair falling down her back, laughing.

Her skin taught, silk to touch. Her lips like wet

fruit.

I bring her carefully wrapped gifts,

prized – exquisite – beautiful objects

jade, pearl, opal.

Objects that delight us, her mouth open

iridescent.

Smiles genuinely – at the thought – IS happy.

And I make her dress as she did that first time.

This is something that we do.

Everything as it was.

It is game we like to play.

She dresses in what she wore that first night.

Everything the same.

She enters my flat.

And we begin again.

As we once where.

I take her coat.

I pour her a drink.

We sit.

She tells me she likes lots of different types of
music.

She tells me there is no type of food she
particularly prefers.

We drink some more.

And then I put my hand around the back of
her neck and she tilts her head
and we kiss.

This makes us laugh together.

She was from Chippenham – a cosy family I
felt, when I met them, with a seedier arm:
an Aunt who lives in Finchley with her criminal
husband, well mostly not with him, inside for
armed robbery – so Judy whispers.

We begin a shared history.
A pattern of living.
Small at first and then it grows.
She never asks.
She does not invade.
She trusts.
Sunday afternoons.
Walks.
Films.
Chinese every other Friday.
She fits herself around me.

And
And

I ask her to marry me. I do sometimes ask
them to marry me.

It is as if a perfect world has been dropped into her lap.

You can touch her joy, her happiness so solid.

Judy is special.

Draping herself willingly
wantonly, somewhere, somehow
knowingly into
the-arms-of-all-of-me.

We are so happy together.
Our jubilation brings attention.
We are praised, a handsome pair,
wherever we go.
I skip.

Such is the quality of our love and her light.

I love.

* * *

On the wedding day her Aunt, the Aunt with
the criminal husband – she comes up to me
and says,

'I hate Northern Soul, the stuff that club of
yours plays; like the Bee Gees, myself. You
know where you are with a bunch of poofs.'

Then she follows me into the gents.

'I know you' she says.
'Do you?' I say.
'I know your type. You know the story of
Bluebeard? Had a chamber didn't he, where
he tortured all his wives to death. Gives his new
wife a gold key that opens it, tells her not to
open it, but then she goes right ahead. So he
tries to kill her too.'

'I don't look good in a beard' I say.

And she says.
'I like it, all that rough against me.'

'You watch it?' She says.
'Watch what?'
'Course you do. Everyone does.
They start watching it when they're twelve now
don't they, earlier if they're boys, so much on
line. Easy. I love a bit of porn – cheers me right
up. You know late at night, well early in the

morning – anytime really. Stops me from
thinking.

You're in the moment – like Buddha says, isn't
that what he's always saying, "feel the now" –
did a course once, trying to find myself or
something. Well, after – the course – you know
when I was watching it – I suddenly thought –
you know like a flash! (*Beat.*)
I'm in the now – then I think, you're always in
the now when you're watching porn. No doubt
about it.

And the girls now, I mean, what an education!
– They know just what to do don't they. They
all do. How to please. All the tricks. You can't
compete with this lot, they've watched too
much porn.' And she laughs, her mouth is
wide, her teeth are very, very white. And her
forehead is ice smooth, not a wrinkle.

'Not me though of course – been there, done
that, got the cardigan . . . There's no known
tricks that I can't do or haven't done, or won't
do'. And she winks. 'Had surgery on my pussy

too, tight as a sixteen year old, and naked as a
new born.'

And then she says this, or near abouts.

'My daughter went into glamour. Went to see
her din' I. In one of those Nuts clubs. You been
to one, course you have. They start on the
poles, dotted round the room, lap dancing.
And there's this bed in the middle and the best
of the girls are chosen for the bed. All sorts of
girls there, educated and that, rich, poor. They
all want it. She looked brilliant on the bed with
her top off, the men loved it. They were
roaring. I was so proud. She wants to do law,
but wants some money behind her first. Got
into Zoo, not that they paid her. She's with an
agency now. Been in Loaded too. Loves it. She
knows what's what. She knows, Jim, can I call
you Jim? Course I can. You're family now. She
knows what's what.'

Though, 'Sophia', her daughter, has got a bit
distracted with the modelling, she's going to
hold over the GCSEs for another year.

'You can't get anywhere unless you know what men want.'

And then she sighs.

'But there are extremes aren't there. I mean I don't mind a bit of slap and tickle, as much as the next man/woman.

But you can go too far. Now you, you.' And she places a hand on my leg.

'You. You might be a bit too far for our Judy. Yeah, bit too much. Reckon she doesn't know what she's chewed off. Fond of Judy I am. Like my own. And I'm always suspicious of the large age gaps – "specially when there's no excuse these days" – I spend thousands on keeping me weather proof. No. Let's be serious.' And her hand rises to the top of my thigh, I can feel it just – touching.

'These very large age gaps – well they hint, don't they, about "mortality" and that. As if looking at her, marrying her, makes you as young, young again; that your "end" Jim, can be pushed further down the line.

Or worse, and this is really what "I am afeard of", worse still – the destruction of it, the

breaking of her, of the young. Like a fucking vampire.' And she laughs again. 'You a fucking vampire, Jim?'
The thing is I don't know which end of the candle you burn, but I can smell you, oh yeah, I can smell you alright.'
And she is very close and then, she leans closer still and kisses me hard. I feel her white, white teeth against mine. She tastes good, all that money on herself well spent.

Then she pulls away. And says, 'We would, wouldn't we.
Let's not.
Bit disrespectful.
On the actual wedding night.'

And we both laugh.

Then she says.

'I killed a man once. He was coming at me, wan' he, with a knife, killed him dead. Shot him just here (*Taps middle of forehead.*) got off though, self-defence wan' it.'

* * *

Judy gives me a letter on the wedding night.

Bluebeard *picks up the letter and reads.*

It has a title – she calls it – 'what you do to me'.

'When I first saw you, walking across the room to me, I felt every part of me burn. Your dark hair, your dark looks, your eyes, your eyes looked inside me, they reached into the middle of me and a flame inside my stomach was lit for the first time, ever.

You are everything to me. You have filled up the great gaping hole inside me. Now I am complete.

I love the way you curl your fingers around my hair.
I love the smell of you, the taste of you.
I love the way you pull my hair back, bending my neck so I can only see you, I love the way you plunge your tongue into my mouth and explore every part of my taste.

I love your hands across me, I love their feel against my skin, I love the strength in your hold. I love your lips, your beautiful lips as they hold my tiny breasts and suck and bite me. I love your fingers across the backs of my legs, across my thighs, pushing my clothes to one side and reaching into me, forcefully, with such certainty.

I love the way you force me to kneel in front of you and take your manhood. I love the edge of harm in you when hold me down, pull my hair and skilfully manoeuvre me about our bed. I love your tongue inside me. I love your cock inside me. I love your silence as you fuck me into oblivion. I love the violence in you, can I say that?

And how you hurt me with your love.

I feel safe with you.

I want you to know this, that I love you so very much, that you, you my dear dark love, on the eve of our wedding night, can do anything to me.'

That's what it says.

Bluebeard *puts letter down.*

But what a let down, what a disappointment.

She starts to ask on that night.

On the wedding night.

About who and what I really am.

Family.

Asks about my past. Ask about my suffering,

my nature.

Digs.

Asks about food.

Opens my torture chamber.

'It's innate isn't it!'

Pities me.

She's like a lamb to the slaughter.

It's easy.

The silk blindfold, the love.

The annihilation wanted – sought – ask for

really.

Her nature – my nature.

The tyrant and the slave.

The strong and the weak.

This paradise is the model of the world – my

chamber.

I tie her down.

I am so hard, so erect, my skip in heaven a
moment away – her death a whisper, a breath
away.

I place my hand across her mouth, she
struggles, giggles,
take the knife and slowly run it down her body,
gently, sweetly, still she twists and turns for that
ached for pleasure.

And then, just now, I turn the blade against
her
and
cut.

She tries to cry out but my hand stops the
sound.
She cannot be heard.

So excited – with quiet sensual pleasure.

Her eyes widen in terror.
I turn the knife again.

Then the fucking door opens.

Her Aunt, with a . . .

FX Gun. **Bluebeard** *clutches his head.*

The bullet shatters my skull.

Through touch, smell, want, memory,
empathy,
vision, colour, light, dark.

Eleven seconds.

One, two, three, four, five, six, seven, eight,
nine, ten.

And now, just now, I die.

Death rattle/breath.

Judy is screaming.

My blood is everywhere
splattered
across the walls of time.

He sits back – takes his time, maybe smiles.

But I know you like it.

I know you see.

I know you prefer the brute.

The Bonds

The Lovelaces

The Valmonts

The Bronsons

The vampires

The wolves

The animals.

Here amongst you, always and forever.

I am.

Never short, you understand, never short of a
woman that wants me.

FX MUSIC 'If you leave me now,' by Chicago. **Bluebeard** *exits.*